CHRISTMAS JOY
for Flute Duet

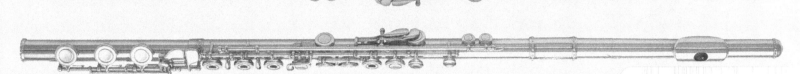

ARRANGED BY JUDY NISHIMURA

ISBN 978-1-5400-2950-8

SHAWNEE PRESS

EXCLUSIVELY DISTRIBUTED BY

HAL•LEONARD®

Visit Shawnee Press Online at
www.shawneepress.com

Visit Hal Leonard Online at
www.halleonard.com

Contact Us:
Hal Leonard
7777 West Bluemound Road
Milwaukee, WI 53213
Email: info@halleonard.com

In Europe contact:
Hal Leonard Europe Limited
Distribution Centre, Newmarket Road
Bury St Edmunds, Suffolk, IP33 3YB
Email: info@halleonardeurope.com

In Australia contact:
Hal Leonard Australia Pty. Ltd.
4 Lentara Court
Cheltenham, Victoria, 3192 Australia
Email: info@halleonard.com.au

ABOUT THE ARRANGER

A lifelong resident of Chicago, **Judy Nishimura** (b. 1953) received her degree in Flute Performance from Northwestern University after studying with Walfrid Kujala of the Chicago Symphony. Her award-winning music for flutes, including a book of flute and piano arrangements entitled *Christmas Jubilation* (Shawnee Press, 2012) have been performed all over the world. In 2015, her original composition "Transverses" won 1st Prize in the National Flute Association's Flute Choir Composition Competition.

ANGELS WE HAVE HEARD ON HIGH

Traditional French Carol
Translated by James Chadwick
Arranged by Judy Nishimura

4

AWAY IN A MANGER

Traditional Lyrics
Music by James R. Murray and William J. Kirkpatrick
Arranged by Judy Nishimura

DING DONG! MERRILY ON HIGH

French Carol
Arranged by Judy Nishimura

THE FIRST NOËL

17th Century English Carol
Music from *W. Sandys' Christmas Carols*
Arranged by Judy Nishimura

HARK! THE HERALD ANGELS SING

Words by Charles Wesley
Music by Felix Mendelssohn-Bartholdy
Arranged by Judy Nishimura

HE IS BORN, THE HOLY CHILD
(Il Est Ne, Le Divine Enfant)

Traditional French Carol
Arranged by Judy Nishimura

I HEARD THE BELLS ON CHRISTMAS DAY

Words by Henry Wadsworth Longfellow
Music by John Baptiste Calkin
Arranged by Judy Nishimura

IN DULCI JUBILO

14th Century German Melody
Arranged by Judy Nishimura

IT CAME UPON THE MIDNIGHT CLEAR

Words by Edmund Hamilton Sears
Music by Richard Storrs Willis
Arranged by Judy Nishimura

JOY TO THE WORLD

Words by Isaac Watts
Music by George Frideric Handel
Arranged by Judy Nishimura

LO, HOW A ROSE E'ER BLOOMING

15th Century German Carol
Music from *Alte Catholische Geistliche Kirchengesanghe*
Arranged by Judy Nishimura

O COME, ALL YE FAITHFUL

Music by John Francis Wade
Latin words translated by Frederick Oakeley
Arranged by Judy Nishimura

O COME, O COME, EMMANUEL

Traditional Latin Text
15th Century French Melody
Arranged by Judy Nishimura

O HOLY NIGHT

French words by Placide Cappeau
English words by John S. Dwight
Music by Adolphe Adam
Arranged by Judy Nishimura

O LITTLE TOWN OF BETHLEHEM

Words by Phillips Brooks
Music by Lewis H. Redner
Arranged by Judy Nishimura

SILENT NIGHT

Words by Joseph Mohr
Music by Franz X. Gruber
Arranged by Judy Nishimura

SING WE NOW OF CHRISTMAS

Traditional French Carol
Arranged by Judy Nishimura

STILL, STILL, STILL

Salzburg Melody, c.1819
Traditional Austrian Text
Arranged by Judy Nishimura

WE WISH YOU A MERRY CHRISTMAS

Traditional English Folksong
Arranged by Judy Nishimura

WHAT CHILD IS THIS?

Words by William C. Dix
16th Century English Melody
Arranged by Judy Nishimura

101 SONGS

BIG COLLECTIONS OF FAVORITE SONGS ARRANGED FOR SOLO INSTRUMENTALISTS.

101 BROADWAY SONGS

00154199 Flute	$14.99
00154200 Clarinet	$14.99
00154201 Alto Sax	$14.99
00154202 Tenor Sax	$14.99
00154203 Tumpet	$14.99
00154204 Horn	$14.99
00154205 Trombone	$14.99
00154206 Violin	$14.99

00154207 Viola.......................................$14.99
00154208 Cello.......................................$14.99

101 DISNEY SONGS

00244104 Flute	$14.99
00244106 Clarinet	$14.99
00244107 Alto Sax	$14.99
00244108 Tenor Sax	$14.99
00244109 Tumpet	$14.99
00244112 Horn	$14.99
00244120 Trombone	$14.99
00244121 Violin	$14.99

00244125 Viola.......................................$14.99
00244126 Cello.......................................$14.99

101 MOVIE HITS

00158087 Flute	$14.99
00158088 Clarinet	$14.99
00158089 Alto Sax	$14.99
00158090 Tenor Sax	$14.99
00158091 Tumpet	$14.99
00158092 Horn	$14.99
00158093 Trombone	$14.99
00158094 Violin	$14.99

00158095 Viola.......................................$14.99
001580 Cello.......................................$14.99

101 CHRISTMAS SONGS

00278637 Flute	$14.99
00278638 Clarinet	$14.99
00278639 Alto Sax	$14.99
00278640 Tenor Sax	$14.99
00278641 Tumpet	$14.99
00278642 Horn	$14.99
00278643 Trombone	$14.99
00278644 Violin	$14.99

00278645 Viola.......................................$14.99
00278646 Cello.......................................$14.99

101 HIT SONGS

00194561 Flute	$14.99
00197182 Clarinet	$14.99
00197183 Alto Sax	$14.99
00197184 Tenor Sax	$14.99
00197185 Tumpet	$14.99
00197186 Horn	$14.99
00197187 Trombone	$14.99
00197188 Violin	$14.99

00197189 Viola.......................................$14.99
00197190 Cello.......................................$14.99

101 POPULAR SONGS

00224722 Flute	$14.99
00224723 Clarinet	$14.99
00224724 Alto Sax	$14.99
00224725 Tenor Sax	$14.99
00224726 Tumpet	$14.99
00224727 Horn	$14.99
00224728 Trombone	$14.99
00224729 Violin	$14.99

00224730 Viola.......................................$14.99
00224731 Cello.......................................$14.99

101 CLASSICAL THEMES

00155315 Flute	$14.99
00155317 Clarinet	$14.99
00155318 Alto Sax	$14.99
00155319 Tenor Sax	$14.99
00155320 Tumpet	$14.99
00155321 Horn	$14.99
00155322 Trombone	$14.99
00155323 Violin	$14.99

00155324 Viola.......................................$14.99
0000155325 Cello.......................................$14.99

101 JAZZ SONGS

00146363 Flute	$14.99
00146364 Clarinet	$14.99
00146366 Alto Sax	$14.99
00146367 Tenor Sax	$14.99
00146368 Tumpet	$14.99
00146369 Horn	$14.99
00146370 Trombone	$14.99
00146371 Violin	$14.99

00146372 Viola.......................................$14.99
00146373 Cello.......................................$14.99

101 MOST BEAUTIFUL SONGS

00291023 Flute	$14.99
00291041 Clarinet	$14.99
00291042 Alto Sax	$14.99
00291043 Tenor Sax	$14.99
00291044 Tumpet	$14.99
00291045 Horn	$14.99
00291046 Trombone	$14.99
00291047 Violin	$14.99

00291048 Viola.......................................$14.99
00291049 Cello.......................................$14.99

See complete song lists and sample pages at www.halleonard.com

HAL•LEONARD®
www.halleonard.com

0121
217

Prices, contents and availability subject to change without notice.

EXCEPTIONAL FLUTE PUBLICATIONS from HAL LEONARD

BIG BOOK OF FLUTE SONGS

Flutists will love this giant collection of 130 popular solos! Includes: Another One Bites the Dust • Any Dream Will Do • Bad Day • Beauty and the Beast • Breaking Free • Clocks • Edelweiss • God Bless the U.S.A. • Heart and Soul • I Will Remember You • Imagine • Na Na Hey Hey Kiss Him Goodbye • Satin Doll • United We Stand • You Raise Me Up • and dozens more!
00842207 $14.95

CLAUDE BOLLING – SUITE FOR FLUTE AND JAZZ PIANO TRIO

This suite in seven parts is composed for a "classic" flute and a "jazz" piano. It was the first jazz recording of world-renowned flutist Jean-Pierre Rampal and Claude Bolling. It is possible to play the whole piece with only flute and piano, but bass and drum parts are included for the complete Suite. The CD includes full recordings and flute play-along tracks for seven songs: Baroque and Blue • Fugace • Irlandaise • Javanaise • Sentimentale • Veloce • Versatile.
00672558 Set of Parts/CD $59.95

THE BOOSEY & HAWKES FLUTE ANTHOLOGY

24 PIECES BY 16 COMPOSERS

Boosey & Hawkes

Intermediate to advanced literature from the Romantic era to the 20th century. Special study paid to various state high school contest solo repertory lists. Contents: Gavotte and Musette from Divertimento (Alwyn) • Scherzo from Suite Paysanne Hongroise (Bartók) • First Movement from Duo for Flute and Piano (Copland) • Vocalise (Copland) • Valentine Piece, Op. 70 (Górecki) • Duo for Two Flutes (Lees) • Rhapsody on a Theme of Paganini, Op. 43 (Rachmaninoff) • and many more.
48019634 $24.99

ÉTUDES MODERNES POUR FLUTE

[MODERN STUDIES FOR FLUTE]

Alphonse Leduc

Modern Studies for the Flute is a set of sixteen studies by Paul Jeanjean (1874-1928). Composed in 1868, and initially composed for clarinet, these studies would fit advanced players. Each one of these *Modern Studies* is 3 or 4 pages long and extremely technically challenging.
48182950 $39.99

FLUTE FINGERING CHART

FOR FLUTE AND PICCOLO

In addition to a detailed fingering chart, this handy laminated fold-out card includes notes about instrument care, transposition, pitch system, and notation. A valuable tool for any flute player!
14011341 $7.95

THE G. SCHIRMER FLUTE ANTHOLOGY

14 WORKS FROM THE 20TH CENTURY

G. Schirmer, Inc.

Selected works from the most prominent G. Schirmer and AMP composers, including music by Barber, Corigliano, Harbison, Martinu, Moyse, Muczynski, and others. With detailed notes on the music. Suitable for the advanced high school and college level player. Includes works for solo flute as well as flute and piano.
50499531 $19.99

IMPROVISATION FOR FLUTE

THE SCALE/MODE APPROACH

by Andy McGhee

Berklee Press

Expand the creative breadth of your soloing! The step-by-step exercises and explanations in this tried-&-true resource will help you develop your ear and improve your technique. You'll learn the intimate relationships between modes and chords, practicing licks and solos that grow out of their underlying harmonies and sound natural.
50449810 $16.99

JAZZ FLUTE ETUDES

Houston Publishing, Inc.

These etudes by Marc Adler will delight both classical and jazz musicians. Marc is an accomplished flutist and composer in both the jazz and classical arenas and is also an experienced educator. These twelve etudes explore each of the twelve keys but at the same time step out into contemporary sounds characteristic of modern jazz and 20th-century classical music, such as whole tone and diminished scales, and colorful chord progressions. Jazz flutists will enjoy his original jazz licks and may want to add some of them to their vocabulary of patterns.
00030442 $14.99

JETHRO TULL – FLUTE SOLOS

AS PERFORMED BY IAN ANDERSON

transcribed by Jeff Rona

Flute solos from 18 Jethro Tull songs have been transcribed for this collection. Songs include: Bungle in the Jungle • Cross-Eyed Mary • Fire at Midnight • Look into the Sun • Nothing Is Easy • Thick as a Brick • The Witch's Promise • and more.
00672547 $15.99

101 FLUTE TIPS

STUFF ALL THE PROS KNOW AND USE

by Elaine Schmidt

Tips, suggestions, advice and other useful information garnered through a lifetime of flute study and professional gigging are all presented in this book with dozens of entries gleaned from first-hand experience. Topics covered include: selecting the right flute for you • finding the right teacher • warm-up exercises • practicing effectively • taking good care of your flute • gigging advice • staying and playing healthy • members of the flute family • extended ranges and techniques • and flute fraternization.
00119883 Book/CD Pack $14.99

HAL•LEONARD®

Prices, contents, and availability subject to change without notice.

0719
214

HAL•LEONARD INSTRUMENTAL PLAY-ALONG

Your favorite songs are arranged just for solo instrumentalists with this outstanding series. Each book includes great full-accompaniment play-along audio so you can sound just like a pro!

Check out **halleonard.com** for songlists, more titles, or to order online from your favorite music retailer.

12 Pop Hits
12 songs • $14.99 each
00261790	Flute	00261795	Horn
00261791	Clarinet	00261796	Trombone
00261792	Alto Sax	00261797	Violin
00261793	Tenor Sax	00261798	Viola
00261794	Trumpet	00261799	Cello

The Very Best of Bach
15 selections • $12.99 each
00225371	Flute	00225376	Horn
00225372	Clarinet	00225377	Trombone
00225373	Alto Sax	00225378	Violin
00225374	Tenor Sax	00225379	Viola
00225375	Trumpet	00225380	Cello

The Beatles
15 songs • $14.99 each
00225330	Flute	00225335	Horn
00225331	Clarinet	00225336	Trombone
00225332	Alto Sax	00225337	Violin
00225333	Tenor Sax	00225338	Viola
00225334	Trumpet	00225339	Cello

Chart Hits
12 songs • $14.99 each
00146207	Flute	00146212	Horn
00146208	Clarinet	00146213	Trombone
00146209	Alto Sax	00146214	Violin
00146210	Tenor Sax	00146215	Viola
00146211	Trumpet	00146216	Cello

Christmas Songs
12 songs • $12.99 each
00146855	Flute	00146863	Horn
00146858	Clarinet	00146864	Trombone
00146859	Alto Sax	00146866	Violin
00146860	Tenor Sax	00146867	Viola
00146862	Trumpet	00146868	Cello

Contemporary Broadway
15 songs • $14.99 each
00298704	Flute	00298709	Horn
00298705	Clarinet	00298710	Trombone
00298706	Alto Sax	00298711	Violin
00298707	Tenor Sax	00298712	Viola
00298708	Trumpet	00298713	Cello

Disney Movie Hits
12 songs • $14.99 each
00841420	Flute	00841424	Horn
00841687	Oboe	00841425	Trombone
00841421	Clarinet	00841426	Violin
00841422	Alto Sax	00841427	Viola
00841686	Tenor Sax	00841428	Cello
00841423	Trumpet		

Disney Solos
12 songs • $14.99 each
00841404	Flute	00841506	Oboe
00841406	Alto Sax	0841409	Trumpet
00841407	Horn	00841410	Violin
00841411	Viola	00841412	Cello
00841405	Clarinet/Tenor Sax		
00841408	Trombone/Baritone		
00841553	Mallet Percussion		

Dixieland Favorites
15 songs • $12.99 each
00268756	Flute	0068759	Trumpet
00268757	Clarinet	00268760	Trombone
00268758	Alto Sax		

Billie Eilish
9 songs • $14.99 each
00345648	Flute	00345653	Horn
00345649	Clarinet	00345654	Trombone
00345650	Alto Sax	00345655	Violin
00345651	Tenor Sax	00345656	Viola
00345652	Trumpet	00345657	Cello

Favorite Movie Themes
13 songs • $14.99 each
00841166	Flute	00841168	Trumpet
00841167	Clarinet	00841170	Trombone
00841169	Alto Sax	00841296	Violin

Gospel Hymns
15 songs • $12.99 each
00194648	Flute	00194654	Trombone
00194649	Clarinet	00194655	Violin
00194650	Alto Sax	00194656	Viola
00194651	Tenor Sax	00194657	Cello
00194652	Trumpet		

Great Classical Themes
15 songs • $12.99 each
00292727	Flute	00292733	Horn
00292728	Clarinet	00292735	Trombone
00292729	Alto Sax	00292736	Violin
00292730	Tenor Sax	00292737	Viola
00292732	Trumpet	00292738	Cello

The Greatest Showman
8 songs • $14.99 each
00277389	Flute	00277394	Horn
00277390	Clarinet	00277395	Trombone
00277391	Alto Sax	00277396	Violin
00277392	Tenor Sax	00277397	Viola
00277393	Trumpet	00277398	Cello

Irish Favorites
31 songs • $12.99 each
00842489	Flute	00842495	Trombone
00842490	Clarinet	00842496	Violin
00842491	Alto Sax	00842497	Viola
00842493	Trumpet	00842498	Cello
00842494	Horn		

Michael Jackson
11 songs • $14.99 each
00119495	Flute	00119499	Trumpet
00119496	Clarinet	00119501	Trombone
00119497	Alto Sax	00119503	Violin
00119498	Tenor Sax	00119502	Accomp.

Jazz & Blues
14 songs • $14.99 each
00841438	Flute	00841441	Trumpet
00841439	Clarinet	00841443	Trombone
00841440	Alto Sax	00841444	Violin
00841442	Tenor Sax		

Jazz Classics
12 songs • $12.99 each
00151812	Flute	00151816	Trumpet
00151813	Clarinet	00151818	Trombone
00151814	Alto Sax	00151819	Violin
00151815	Tenor Sax	00151821	Cello

Les Misérables
13 songs • $14.99 each
00842292	Flute	00842297	Horn
00842293	Clarinet	00842298	Trombone
00842294	Alto Sax	00842299	Violin
00842295	Tenor Sax	00842300	Viola
00842296	Trumpet	00842301	Cello

Metallica
12 songs • $14.99 each
02501327	Flute	02502454	Horn
02501339	Clarinet	02501329	Trombone
02501332	Alto Sax	02501334	Violin
02501333	Tenor Sax	02501335	Viola
02501330	Trumpet	02501338	Cello

Motown Classics
15 songs • $12.99 each
00842572	Flute	00842576	Trumpet
00842573	Clarinet	00842578	Trombone
00842574	Alto Sax	00842579	Violin
00842575	Tenor Sax		

Pirates of the Caribbean
16 songs • $14.99 each
00842183	Flute	00842188	Horn
00842184	Clarinet	00842189	Trombone
00842185	Alto Sax	00842190	Violin
00842186	Tenor Sax	00842191	Viola
00842187	Trumpet	00842192	Cello

Queen
17 songs • $14.99 each
00285402	Flute	00285407	Horn
00285403	Clarinet	00285408	Trombone
00285404	Alto Sax	00285409	Violin
00285405	Tenor Sax	00285410	Viola
00285406	Trumpet	00285411	Cello

Simple Songs
14 songs • $12.99 each
00249081	Flute	00249087	Horn
00249092	Oboe	00249089	Trombone
00249082	Clarinet	00249090	Violin
00249083	Alto Sax	00249091	Viola
00249084	Tenor Sax	00249092	Cello
00249086	Trumpet	00249094	Mallets

Superhero Themes
14 songs • $14.99 each
00363195	Flute	00363200	Horn
00363196	Clarinet	00363201	Trombone
00363197	Alto Sax	00363202	Violin
00363198	Tenor Sax	00363203	Viola
00363199	Trumpet	00363204	Cello

Star Wars
16 songs • $16.99 each
00350900	Flute	00350907	Horn
00350913	Oboe	00350908	Trombone
00350903	Clarinet	00330909	Violin
00350904	Alto Sax	00350910	Viola
00350905	Tenor Sax	00350911	Cello
00350906	Trumpet	00350914	Mallet

Taylor Swift
15 songs • $12.99 each
00842532	Flute	00842537	Horn
00842533	Clarinet	00842538	Trombone
00842534	Alto Sax	00842539	Violin
00842535	Tenor Sax	00842540	Viola
00842536	Trumpet	00842541	Cello

Video Game Music
13 songs • $12.99 each
00283877	Flute	00283883	Horn
00283878	Clarinet	00283884	Trombone
00283879	Alto Sax	00283885	Violin
00283880	Tenor Sax	00283886	Viola
00283882	Trumpet	00283887	Cello

Wicked
13 songs • $12.99 each
00842236	Flute	00842241	Horn
00842237	Clarinet	00842242	Trombone
00842238	Alto Sax	00842243	Violin
00842239	Tenor Sax	00842244	Viola
00842240	Trumpet	00842245	Cello

Prices, contents, and availability subject to change without notice.

Disney characters and artwork ™ & © 2021 Disney

HAL•LEONARD®

Hal·Leonard Classical PLAY-ALONG™

The Hal Leonard Classical Play-Along™ series will help you play great classical pieces. Listen to the full performance tracks to hear how the piece sounds with an orchestra, and then play along using the accompaniment tracks. The audio CD is playable on any CD player. For PC and Mac computer users, the CD is enhanced so you can adjust the recording to any tempo without changing pitch.

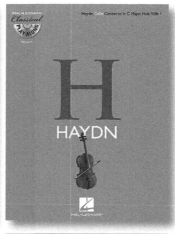

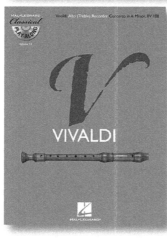

1. MOZART:
FLUTE CONCERTO IN D MAJOR, K314
Book/CD Pack
00842341 Flute......................$12.99

2. SAMMARTINI:
DESCANT (SOPRANO) RECORDER
CONCERTO IN F MAJOR
Book/CD Pack
00842342 Soprano Recorder......................$12.99

3. LOEILLET:
TREBLE (ALTO) RECORDER
SONATA IN G MAJOR, OP.1, NO.3
Book/CD Pack
00842343 Alto Recorder......................$12.99

4. MOZART:
CLARINET CONCERTO IN A MAJOR, K622
Book/CD Pack
00842344 Clarinet......................$12.99

6. MOZART:
HORN CONCERTO IN D MAJOR, K412/514
Book/CD Pack
00842346 Horn......................$12.99

7. BACH:
VIOLIN CONCERTO IN A MINOR, BWV 1041
Book/CD Pack
00842347 Violin......................$12.99

8. TELEMANN:
VIOLA CONCERTO IN G MAJOR, TWV 51:G9
Book/Online Audio
00842348 Viola......................$12.99

9. HAYDN:
CELLO CONCERTO IN C MAJOR, HOB.
VIIB: 1
Book/CD Pack
00842349 Cello......................$12.99

10. BACH:
PIANO CONCERTO IN F MINOR, BWV 1056
Book/CD Pack
00842350 Piano......................$12.99

11. PERGOLESI:
FLUTE CONCERTO IN G MAJOR
Book/CD Pack
00842351 Flute......................$12.99

12. BARRE:
DESCANT (SOPRANO) RECORDER
SUITE NO. 9 "DEUXIEME LIVRE" G MAJOR
Book/Online Audio
00842352 Soprano Recorder......................$12.99

14. VON WEBER:
CLARINET CONCERTO NO. 1 IN F MINOR,
OP. 73
Book/CD Pack
00842354 Clarinet......................$12.99

15. MOZART:
VIOLIN CONCERTO IN G MAJOR, K216
Book/CD Pack
00842355 Violin......................$12.99

16. BOCCHERINI:
CELLO CONCERTO IN B-FLAT MAJOR,
G482
Book/CD Pack
00842356 Cello......................$12.99

17. MOZART:
PIANO CONCERTO IN C MAJOR, K467
Book/CD Pack
00842357 Piano......................$12.99

18. BACH:
FLUTE SONATA IN E-FLAT MAJOR,
BWV 1031
Book/CD Pack
00842450 Flute......................$12.99

19. BRAHMS:
CLARINET SONATA IN F MINOR, OP. 120,
NO. 1
Book/CD Pack
00842451 Clarinet......................$12.99

20. BEETHOVEN:
TWO ROMANCES FOR VIOLIN,
OP. 40 IN G & OP. 50 IN F
Book/CD Pack
00842452 Violin......................$12.99

21. MOZART:
PIANO CONCERTO IN D MINOR, K466
Book/CD Pack
00842453 Piano......................$12.99

Prices, content, and availability subject to change without notice.

www.halleonard.com